7/16 $29

597
RAUM

Raum, Elizabeth
Stonefish

Stonefish

BY ELIZABETH RAUM

AMICUS HIGH INTEREST ✦ AMICUS INK

Amicus High Interest and Amicus Ink are imprints of Amicus
P.O. Box 1329, Mankato, MN 56002
www.amicuspublishing.us

Library of Congress Cataloging-in-Publication Data
Raum, Elizabeth.
 Stonefish / by Elizabeth Raum.
    pages cm. – (Poisonous animals)
 Summary: "This photo-illustrated book for elementary readers
describes the poisonous stonefish. Readers learn how these
ocean animals use stingers on their backs to defend against
predators. Also explains the threat of these stings to humans
and what to do when stonefish are encountered"– Provided
by publisher.
 Audience: K to Grade 3.
 Includes index.
 ISBN 978-1-60753-790-8 (library binding)
 ISBN 978-1-60753-889-9 (ebook)
 ISBN 978-1-68152-041-4 (paperback)
 1. Stonefishes–Juvenile literature. I. Title.
 QL638.S42R38 2016
 597'.68–dc23

                                        2014038747

Editor: Wendy Dieker
Series Designer: Kathleen Petelinsek
Book Designer: Heather Dreisbach
Photo Researcher: Derek Brown

Photo Credits: OceanwideImages cover; Ethan Daniels/
Shutterstock 5; Clay Bryce/SeaPics.com 6; Blend Images/
Alamy 9; Vibrant Image Studio/Shutterstock 10; Hemis/
Alamy 12-13; RGB Ventures/SuperStock/Alamy 14;
Poelzer Wolfgang/Alamy 17; LauraD/Shutterstock 18;
orlandin/Shutterstock 21; John A. Anderson/Shutterstock
22; frantisekhojdysz/Shutterstock 24-25; Anna Jurkovska/
Shutterstock 26; DigiPub/Getty Images 29

HC 10 9 8 7 6 5 4 3 2
PB 10 9 8 7 6 5 4 3 2 1

Table of Contents

It's Not a Rock!

The stonefish lies in shallow water. It looks like a rock. A woman wades into the water. She steps on a rock. Stop! It's not a rock. It's a stonefish! When it is disturbed, it raises sharp spines on its back. A spine enters her foot. The pain is terrible. If she doesn't get help, she will die.

Stonefish are hard to see in the water. They look just like rocks!

Look closely at the spines along the stonefish's back.

 How strong is stonefish **venom**?

The stonefish has thirteen sharp spines on its back. Most of the time, the spines lie flat. They pop up when the stonefish is upset. When people step on a stonefish, the spines pierce their feet. The spines send venom into the wound. It is strong venom. The stonefish is the deadliest fish in the sea.

It can kill a person in less than an hour.

Pouring hot water on the wound helps. But anyone who steps on a stonefish must see a doctor. Stonefish venom causes **infections**. It attacks the heart. In the past, many people died. Today, doctors have medicine called **antivenin**. It saves lives. However, the wounds may take months to heal.

 Do stonefish attack people?

If you are stung by a stonefish, see a doctor right away.

 No. They just want to be left alone.

Are there stonefish hiding in the rocks on this beach?

A Closer Look

Stonefish live in **tropical** ocean waters. They live in the Indian Ocean. They are found on the coasts of Africa, Australia, and Southeast Asia. Stonefish live in shallow water near the beach. They hide among coral, rocks, rubble, or sea plants. They often bury themselves in the sand.

There are about 20 different **species**, or kinds, of stonefish. Stonefish are not big. Most are 12 to 15 inches (30 to 38 cm) long. A few grow to almost 20 inches (51 cm). Their bodies are shaped like triangles. Stonefish have small eyes and big mouths.

If a stonefish decides to move, big fins push it through the water.

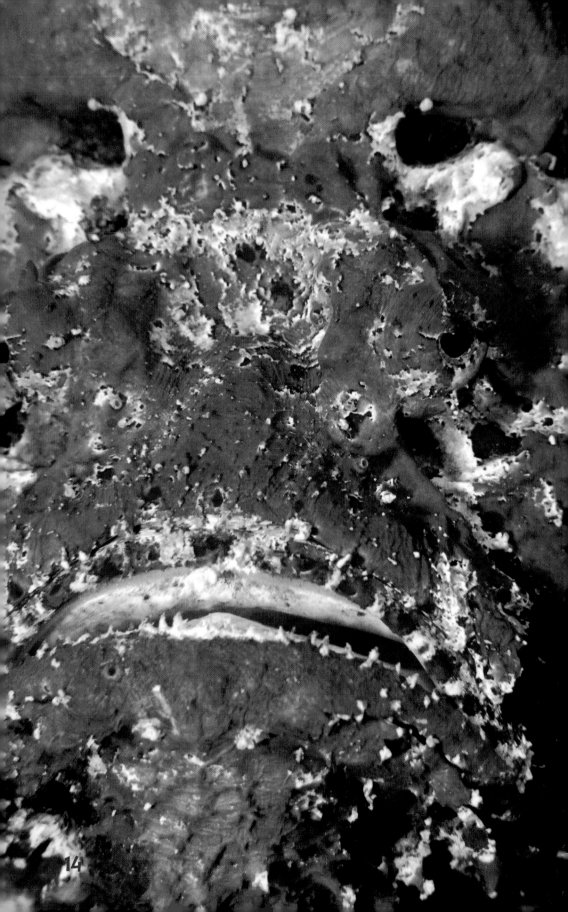

Stonefish do not have scales. Instead, they have rough skin. Most stonefish are brown or grey. They may have patches of yellow, orange, or red. Stonefish are not rare. But few people ever see them. Their color helps them hide. They remain still for a long time.

Some stonefish are pink to blend in with pink coral.

Waiting for Lunch

A hungry stonefish burrows into the sand or mud. It waits for **prey**. It may wait for hours. The stonefish doesn't move. A small fish swims by. The stonefish's mouth snaps open. The stonefish sucks the prey into its mouth and swallows it. In a flash, the prey disappears.

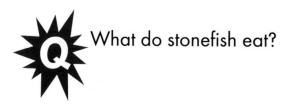 What do stonefish eat?

The white inside a stonefish's mouth shows when it opens wide to suck in food.

 They eat small fish and shrimp.

Can you see the stonefish
waiting in this dry tide pool?

Sometimes the stonefish sits on the ocean bottom. Other times it stays in shallow water. If the **tide** goes out, the stonefish is stuck on land. Most fish die on land. Not the stonefish. It can stay out of the water for hours. It just waits until the tide comes in. Then it can eat again.

Staying Alive

Most stonefish stay near coral reefs. They may live in shallow tide pools and under rocky ledges. Stonefish are not strong swimmers. Their bodies are heavy. They use their fins to help them move around on the ocean floor. But they are too slow to swim away from their enemies.

 Q Which animals try to hunt stonefish?

Coral reefs are filled with animals. Snake eels like this swim near stonefish.

 Sharks, stingrays, and sea snakes will eat them.

Predators look for fish to eat. But stonefish are **camouflaged**. They blend in with the coral. Some look like rocks. Others look like plants. Often, stonefish will bury themselves in the sand. Only their mouth or eyes show above the sand. The stonefish lie still. Predators can't see them. Enemies pass right by.

Green algae grows on some stonefish. They really look like the rocks around them!

Stonefish use their venom for defense. It doesn't always help. Sharks and stingrays search the ocean bottom for food. Sometimes they find a stonefish. They swallow it in one big bite. Some sea snakes eat stonefish, too. The venom will not hurt them unless they are stung.

Large sharks can eat stonefish without getting stung.

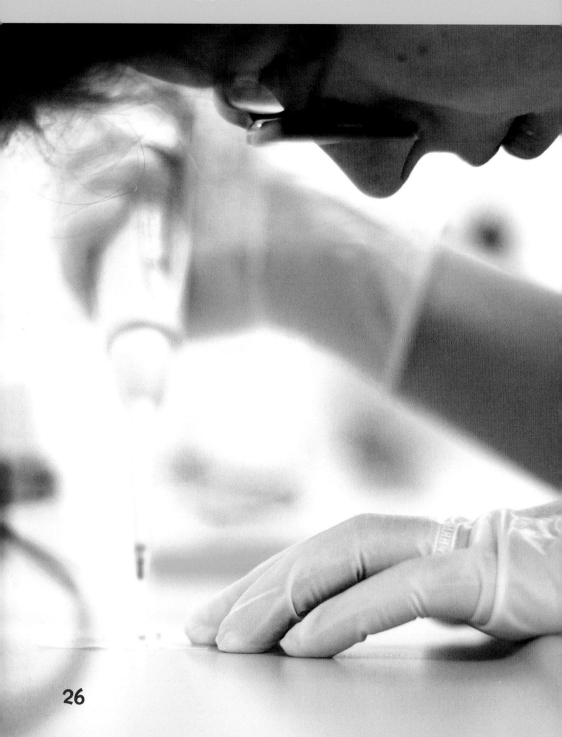

Studying stonefish venom may help find cures for other types of venom.

Good News

Someday, stonefish may save lives. Scientists in Australia study stonefish in labs. They use special gloves to collect venom. Scientists think that stonefish venom may help them make antivenin for box jellyfish stings. Every year many people die of box jelly stings. There is no medicine for these stings yet.

Would you like to eat stonefish? Some people do. Japanese chefs use stonefish to make a dish called sashimi. First, the chef removes the poisonous spines. Then he cuts the stonefish meat, stomach, and skin into thick slices. He serves it raw. It tastes fresh and chewy. The liver tastes salty. No wonder sharks like it!

 Is it safe to eat stonefish?

These stonefish might become a tasty meal!

Yes. Only the spines contain poison. There is no poison in the meat.

Glossary

antivenin Medicine used to treat stonefish wounds.

camouflage Having coloring that helps an animal blend in with their surroundings.

infection When germs enter a wound and do damage, making a person sick.

prey An animal that is hunted for food.

species A kind or group of animals that share certain characteristics.

tide The change in sea level caused by the pull of the sun and moon on the earth.

tropical Warmer waters near the Earth's equator.

venom Poison produced by some animals, like stonefish.

Read More

Antill, Sara. *Stonefish*. New York: Windmill Books, 2011.

Goldish, Meish. *Stonefish: Needles of Pain*. New York: Bearport Pub., 2010.

Shea, Nicole. *Creepy Sea Creatures*. New York: Gareth Stevens Pub., 2012.

Websites

Dangerous Encounters: Deadly Stonefish | National Geographic
channel.nationalgeographic.com/wild/dangerous-encounters/videos/deadly-stone-fish/

Easy Science for Kids | All About Poisonous Fish
http://easyscienceforkids.com/all-about-poisonous-fish/

Stonefish Venom | Animal Planet
www.animalplanet.com/tv-shows/other/videos/wild-recon-stonefish-venom

Index

About the Author

Elizabeth Raum has worked as a teacher, librarian, and writer. She enjoyed doing research and learning about poisonous animals, but she hopes never to find any of them near her house! Visit her website at www.elizabethraum.net.